W9-BPS-873

Date: 6/21/11

BR 567.91 PEN
Penner, Lucille Recht.
Dinosaur babies /

Dear Parent:

Congratulations! Your child is taking the first steps on an exciting journey. The destination? Independent reading!

STEP INTO READING® will help your child get there. The program offers five steps to reading success. Each step includes fun stories and colorful art. There are also Step into Reading Sticker Books, Step into Reading Math Readers, Step into Reading Write-In Readers, Step into Reading Phonics Readers, and Step into Reading Phonics First Steps! Boxed Sets—a complete literacy program with something for every child.

Learning to Read, Step by Step!

Ready to Read Preschool–Kindergarten
• big type and easy words • rhyme and rhythm • picture clues
For children who know the alphabet and are eager to begin reading.

Reading with Help Preschool–Grade 1
• basic vocabulary • short sentences • simple stories
For children who recognize familiar words and sound out new words with help.

Reading on Your Own Grades 1–3
• engaging characters • easy-to-follow plots • popular topics
For children who are ready to read on their own.

Reading Paragraphs Grades 2–3
• challenging vocabulary • short paragraphs • exciting stories
For newly independent readers who read simple sentences with confidence.

Ready for Chapters Grades 2–4
• chapters • longer paragraphs • full-color art
For children who want to take the plunge into chapter books but still like colorful pictures.

STEP INTO READING® is designed to give every child a successful reading experience. The grade levels are only guides. Children can progress through the steps at their own speed, developing confidence in their reading, no matter what their grade.

Remember, a lifetime love of reading starts with a single step!

To Jaya
–L.R.P.

With thanks to
Dr. Glenn Storrs of
the Yale-Peabody
Museum.

Text copyright © 1991 by Lucille Recht Penner. Illustrations copyright © 1991 by Peter Barrett. All rights reserved under
International and Pan-American Copyright Conventions. Published in the United States by Random House Children's Books,
a division of Random House, Inc., New York, and simultaneously in Canada by Random House of Canada Limited, Toronto.

www.stepintoreading.com
Educators and librarians, for a variety of teaching tools, visit us at www.randomhouse.com/teachers

Library of Congress Cataloging-in-Publication Data
Penner, Lucille Recht. Dinosaur babies / by Lucille Recht Penner ; illustrated by Peter Barrett.   p.   cm. — (Step into reading.
A step 2 book)   Originally published: New York : Random House, c1991. SUMMARY: Describes the characteristics and behavior
of baby dinosaurs. ISBN 0-679-81207-5 (trade) — ISBN 0-679-91207-X (lib. bdg.) 1. Dinosaurs—Infancy—Juvenile literature.
[1. Dinosaurs. 2. Animals—Infancy.] I. Barrett, Peter, 1935– ill.   II. Title.   III. Series: Step into reading. Step 2 book.
QE861.5 .P45   2003   567.9—dc21   2002013646

Printed in the United States of America   50 49 48

STEP INTO READING, RANDOM HOUSE, and the Random House colophon are registered trademarks of Random House, Inc.

STEP INTO READING®

STEP 2

DINOSAUR BABIES

by Lucille Recht Penner

illustrated by Peter Barrett

Random House 🏠 New York

Squeak! Squeak!
Is that the sound
of a baby dinosaur
calling to its mother?

Apatosaurus
(a-PAT-uh-sor-us)

Nobody knows.

Nobody has ever heard
a baby dinosaur.

Nobody has seen one.

All the dinosaurs died millions of years ago. But we know a lot about them from what dinosaur hunters have found...

footprints

teeth

bones

They have found small
baby bones in nests.

They have even found
dinosaur eggs.
Many dinosaurs were very big.
But their eggs were small.

The smallest was only
as big as a quarter.

The biggest was about
the size of a football!

Were dinosaurs good mothers?
This kind of dinosaur was.
She made a nest of mud
and laid her eggs in it.
Chickens sit on their eggs.

Maiasaura
(my-uh-SOR-uh)

But this dinosaur did not.

She was too heavy.

The eggs would break!

She put leaves on the eggs

to keep them warm.

The mother watched the nest.
Lots of animals liked to eat
dinosaur eggs!
She kept them away.

Inside the eggs
the babies grew.
They breathed through
tiny holes in the eggshells.

Troödon
(TRO-o-don)

One day the eggs cracked!

Little baby dinosaurs came out.

They were hungry.

Maybe they squeaked.

The mother dinosaur
brought them food.
The babies ate and ate
all day long.

Dinosaur babies

had big heads and big eyes.

They could see and hear well.

Psittacosaurus
(SIT-uh-ko-SOR-us)

Tyrannosaurus
(tie-RAN-uh-SOR-us)

Human babies are born

without any teeth.

Not dinosaur babies!

They had lots of teeth.

Apatosaurus
(a-PAT-uh-sor-us)

What did baby dinosaurs eat?
Some kinds ate leaves and
berries and seeds.

Some kinds ate little animals
and bugs.

Deinonychus
(die-NON-ee-kus)

Was it safe for baby dinosaurs to hunt for food alone? No! Enemies were all around. And baby dinosaurs could not fight or run fast. They could only hide.

Tyrannosaurus
(tie-RAN-uh-SOR-us)

Some baby dinosaurs were lucky.

Triceratops
(try-SER-uh-tops)

They were never alone.
They lived in herds.

Even then enemies

tried to grab

the babies and eat them!

So the dinosaurs made a circle.

Little ones stayed on the inside.

Big ones guarded the outside.

Babies were safe
in the dinosaur herd.

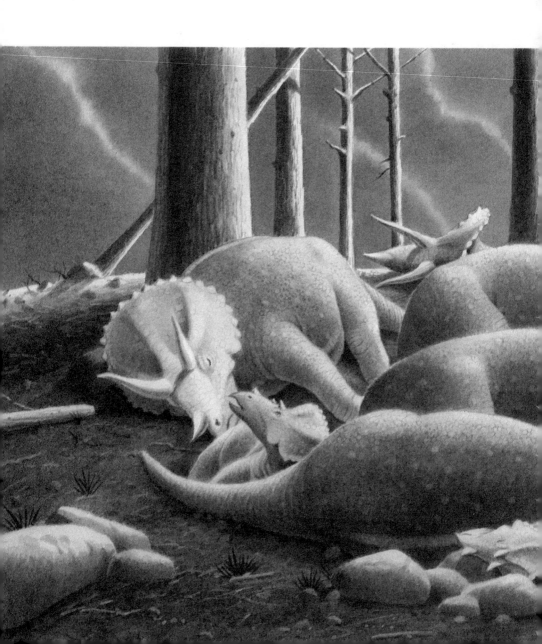

The dinosaurs walked and ate and slept together.

Baby dinosaurs kept growing and changing.

Styracosaurus
(sty-RAK-uh-SOR-us)

Some kinds grew sharp horns.

Some kinds grew spikes
on their tails.

Stegosaurus
(STEG-uh-SOR-us)

Others grew bony frills.

Protoceratops
(PRO-tuh-SER-uh-tops)

Brachiosaurus
(BRAY-kee-uh-SOR-us)

They grew until
they weren't babies
anymore.
Some grew to be the
biggest animals ever
to walk the earth!

And some had
dinosaur babies
of their own.